Your dream is your perfection.

All things are possible!

THE SUCCESS CYCLE

transform dreams into reality

JASON ROMERO

Onward!

—Jason

For the dreamers, pioneers & outcasts
who dare to go where the masses will not,

ONWARD!

Published in the United States by I Am Possible Books

ISBN (paperback): 978-1-7372189-0-6
ISBN (e-book): 978-1-7372189-1-3
ISBN (audiobook): 978-1-7372189-2-0

Art credits:
Cover design: Sierra Romero Graphic Design
Author photos: Gretchen Pilcher (pilcherphotography.com)

THE SUCCESS CYCLE

CONTENTS

PREFACE

All things are possible.

Wait! Is that a zebra?

It can't be! It's 4:30 am, I am at 11,000' elevation in the mountains, freezing, sobbing because of intense physical pain, my legs burn then give out, my back aches from carrying a pack, my stomach is in knots dry heaving into the back of my throat. I think I lost control of my bowels. I feel like the only relief is death. I am 80+ miles into the famed Leadville 100 Trail Race climbing the dreaded Powerline. My feet feel like hammers are crushing them with every step. I stop to catch my breath every few moments. A runner passes me as if they possessed super human powers. I do not.

I hear something from behind me. It's the *grim reaper*, a race volunteer on an ATV. When the ATV reaches me the volunteer speaks,

You have 6 miles and 35 minutes to make it to the next aid station before the cut-off.

I do the math in my head and it is not possible for me to run that fast at altitude in the dark on technical terrain. I fall apart and cry profusely. My dream to finish a 100-mile foot race is over. Shamefully, I mount the ATV and accept a ride to the next aid station. I have DNF'd ("did not finish") the race. Not only that, this DNF was the icing on the cake of a failed Leadman attempt. Leadman is a series of events that takes place in Leadville, Colorado each summer. In order to be a Leadman, you must complete 5 events within specified time cut-offs – the trail marathon, 50-mile mountain bike ride or 50-mile trail run, 100-mile mountain bike ride, 10k run and 100-mile trail run. I had already DNF'd the 100-mile mountain bike ride, finishing an hour after the cut-off. On top of all this failure in Leadville, I was in the midst of a messy divorce and going blind due to a degenerative eye disease. I was 40 years old.

Why at times do we fail and other times succeed? And, are these mutually exclusive results or part of the same process?

In the ensuing 10-years I took on many more challenges personally and professionally. I learned that there is a common process for how success is achieved, and that was the inspiration for this book.

Almost 10-years after that first failed attempt at Leadville, I have completed the Leadville 100-mile run five times, completed Leadman (adding in two additional events – the 50-mile run and 100-mile mountain bike stage race), the Badwater Ultramaration (135 mile run in Death Valley), Spartathlon (153 mile run from Athens to Sparta in Greece), 20+ runs of 100 miles or longer, multiple IronMan triathlons, logged a top-10 fastest foot crossing of the USA (3,063 miles averaging 51.5 miles/day), established and hold several world records and have been a national marathon champion and Paralympian on Team USA. I've been a CEO, attorney, and entrepreneur. In the pursuit of these accomplishments I have failed many times; too many to count.

I discovered there is a process for success; I call it The Success Cycle. The process contained in this book is how I have learned to succeed, and how many extraordinary people succeed. It is not magical and does not come in a pill. Armed with the knowledge contained in this writing, a fervent belief in a dream and the commitment to put forth the requisite effort, you have the ability to realize any dream you can imagine.

ONWARD!

1

SHIFT THE PARADIGM

Success is never ending.

In order to make quantum leaps forward, it is necessary to think in unconventional ways. The Success Cycle is no different, and you will need to change the way you think about some fundamental experiences. This begins with how we define and perceive success.

Success is a cycle and not linear.

LINEAR SUCCESS

Success is not a zero-sum game.

From an early age, we are taught that success is winning. It begins early in life with experiences like field day in elementary school. Most of us have experienced running side-by-side with our peers in a sprint for 50 yards. The person who crossed the finish line first was the victor and this implied success. They received a blue ribbon to signal to all their peers and adults. that they were

LINEAR
SUCCESS

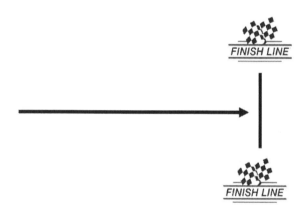

successful in the competition. Unfortunately, the 50-yard dash has become a metaphor for what we have been taught about success.

Success is all too often described and experienced as a linear process.

In this mindset, the process is very simple. You know exactly where the start line is, you can see exactly where the course is, and you know where the finish line is located. Let's look at a Personal and Business example to better understand this concept.

PERSONAL EXAMPLE - Assume it is January 1st, and you have resolved to lose ten pounds. In a "linear mindset," the start line is your current weight. The race course probably looks like some exercise and healthier eating choices. The finish line is when you are ten pounds lighter.

BUSINESS EXAMPLE - Let's say you own a small retail store with a goal to increase sales revenue by 10% as compared to last year. In a "linear mindset," the start line is your annual sales revenue for last fiscal year. The race course probably looks like some plans to grow sales from existing customers, attract new customer sales and minimize losing sales from existing customers. The finish line is when the fiscal year ends and your sales revenue is 10% more than last year.

These seem to be fairly straightforward examples, with conventional thinking. But what happens when you can't seem to stay on track with an exercise schedule, and your sweet tooth consistently has a mind of its own? Day after day, you get on the scale, but you're not getting any closer to your finish line. At times, you may feel like you're actually moving farther away from the finish line, retreating towards the starting line. In the business example, what happens when a new competitor enters the market with a different sales platform (e.g., a gigantic online retailer with free shipping and returns), which disrupts your current brick and mortar business model? Your sales revenue may be significantly impacted, and the finish line of a 10% year-over-year revenue increase may become seemingly unachievable.

This is where conventional thinking breaks down because *success is not a zero-sum game.* The possible outcomes for linear thinking are two-fold, either 1. cross the finish line and succeed, or 2. do not cross the finish line and fail. Thinking about success this way is linear and flawed.

Shift your paradigm to manifest your dreams.

CYCLICAL SUCCESS

Success is judged by the journey,
not the end result.

Success is not about crossing the finish line. Success is a process that may include crossing the finish line. And, the process of success contemplates and includes failure. You may be scratching your head right about now, and thinking "how can this be?"

Success is actually a cyclical process. I developed this cycle from my "Triple A" strategy that I used to overcome a blinding eye disease, solve difficult business situations I encountered as an executive for Fortune 100 companies, become a Paralympian, establish and set World Records and run 3,063 miles across the United States, where I averaged 51.5 miles/day with no days off.

> When there is an *adversity*,
> you must *adapt* in order to *achieve*.

The cyclical process of success has three distinct phases – *adversity, adapt* and *achieve*, with an optional and frequent 4th phase – *the resilience loop*. The cycle begins with adversity which is part of a goal or dream. The second phase of the process is about adapting in order to overcome adversity. If the adversity was not that difficult and adaptations were effective, you will move on to the third phase and achieve your goal or dream. However, if the adversity is very difficult and your adaptations ineffective, you may fail. When you fail, you enter a different part of The Success Cycle called the resilience loop, which is where you will grow stronger, smarter and re-adapt to overcome your dream's adversities. This may sound confusing, but it is not. This is what I call The Success Cycle, and you will be taught the process in detail and simple terms in this book.

CYCLICAL
SUCCESS

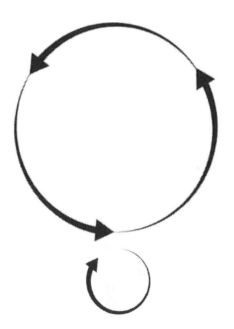

Let's take a closer look at the personal and business situations previously discussed. Your personal goal was to lose ten pounds. Two adversities are your current exercise and eating habits. You adapt to those adversities by creating plans to modify and change those habits. However, you have a tough time following through on incorporating exercise and healthier eating, and you fail to achieve your goal of losing 10 pounds. The process and your quest for success is by no means over. You are now in the resilience loop, an optional sub-process of The Success Cycle, which begins at the end of the adaptation phase. Your adaptations were not able to overcome the adversities, and now you need to re-adapt. You will learn from your mistakes and modify your prior plans, follow through better on your plans, or both. Then, you will execute a new and improved plan. You may find yourself in the resilience loop several times until your adaptations can effectively overcome your adversities, and you are able to lose 10 pounds.

Now, let's turn to the business example where your goal was to grow sales revenue by 10% compared to the prior year. A couple of adversities were customers purchasing habits and market conditions. Your adaptations were focused on customer purchasing habits (i.e., grow sales from existing customers, attract new customers and minimize losing sales from existing customers) and did not anticipate changing market conditions (i.e., the entry of a dominant online retailer becoming a direct competitor). Let's assume you did not achieve your goal of growing revenue by 10% compared to the prior year. You will enter the resilience loop at this point and re-adapt to the adversities until you achieve your dream. In the resilience loop, you will analyze what happened, learn from it, re-adapt and create a plan to overcome adversity. It may take several iterations of re-adapting - failing -learning - re-adapting to overcome adversities, but eventually, you will.

Everything and anything can be achieved using this process. It is simple in concept, although there are some intricacies which I will explain in the following chapters. And finally, a process does not drive itself. You need "fuel" to keep moving through this process and stay energized to keep pursuing your dreams. The *pillars of mental strength* and *biological imperatives* are the fuel you will need to master and practice in order to continue cycling through the process.

Choose to change how you experience success, and you will change your life.

Success is cyclical.

2

BELIEVE THE DREAM

No dream is too large or small to be realized.

In the context of The Success Cycle, the *dream* is the genesis of the process. It is your goal to accomplish, your mission to pursue and your desire to manifest. It is something that sets your wheels in motion and ignites your passion. Why do dreams create such a fervent desire to take action? The answer is readily apparent when a dream is broken down into its constituent components.

A core building block of a dream is a *thought*. And what is a thought? It is the intangible manifestation of a tangible biochemical phenomenon in our brain, which is comprised of trillions of neurons and neurotransmitters that are made up of molecules, which in their most basic form is an atom with electrons, neutrons and protons. Thoughts do not take up matter or space as a rock does. It cannot be held in a hand, or captured with a net. A thought has no physical property and does not take up space in the universe.

THOUGHT

+

BELIEF

=

DREAM

A thought is not matter, but it does matter.

How then does a thought become a dream? A dream is much more than just a thought. A dream is a thought that a person *believes* can become true. A thought without belief is just that, only a thought. The power of human desire, passion and fervor are what ignite a simple thought into a magnificent dream.

The first step in The Success Cycle is to have a defined dream that can be manifested into the material world. It could be for a personal, professional or spiritual pursuit. When you choose to believe in a thought, you set many things into motion and your dream will take on a life of its own. Your dream wants to enter the material world. As you tell more people about your dream, you will notice that more and more people want to help your dream become a reality, and momentum is created. In *The Alchemist*, Paolo Coelho surmised that the universe conspires to help your dreams come true. A dream can take on a life of its own, but it is your undying belief in the thought that breathes life into the dream. Without your belief, a dream will wither and be buried in the cemetery of orphaned thoughts.

Thoughts are talked about randomly during conversations. When dreams are discussed in conversations, listeners are captivated by the dreamer as they describe their dream, with an emphatic voice and glistening eyes. The only way to have a dream is to truly *believe* that a thought can become a reality. This type of belief requires courage, authenticity and vulnerability.

For purposes of demonstrating and explaining concepts in this book, I am going to arbitrarily use a dream of learning to ride a bicycle as a relatable experience. Most people have learned this skill by adulthood, but if you are a person who has not, it is not my intent to disenfranchise you. Please carry on with me, as it will become readily apparent that The Success Cycle process can be generalized to all dreams.

In the past, you may have witnessed another person riding a bicycle, and that may have sparked your curiosity. At some point, you may have developed a thought that it looked fun and interesting, and maybe someday you might learn to ride a bicycle. The dream does not exist yet. The thought of maybe, one day learning to ride a bike is not enough to spur you into action.

This thought will become a dream when you *choose* to *believe* in the *thought*. At some point in your life, you will say to yourself; *I am going to learn to ride a bicycle.* Once you make a choice to believe in your thought, you will create a dream for yourself. At this point, you have initiated The Success Cycle and begun the process.

3

ADVERSITY

Adversity gives us the opportunity
to amaze ourselves on a daily basis.

Inherent in all dreams is adversity - a challenge or obstacle which prevents the dream from becoming a reality. If adversity did not exist, the dream would automatically be fulfilled and manifest into reality of its own volition. Remember, your dreams want to manifest into the material world. Human action is a prerequisite and necessary tool to overcome a dream's adversities.

Once you have defined your dream, you will soon identify adversities or challenges that are impeding your dream from moving forward. It is important to analyze and understand what adversities are obstructing progress toward realizing your dream. Sometimes adversities are complex and difficult, or simple and easy. Some will be internal – within yourself or organization - and others will be external – outside of you or your organization. Adversities are merely situations that prevent your dream from being fulfilled.

ADVERSITY

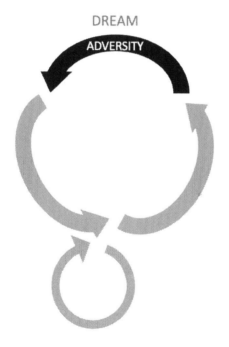

In your effort to learn to ride a bicycle, you are going to confront many adversities. Several illustrations of possible adversities include:

INTERNAL ADVERSITIES
You have limited spare time
You have poor balance
You are scared to crash and be hurt

EXTERNAL ADVERSITIES
No safe place to learn
It is winter and cold outside
Your bike has a flat tire

This list is not exhaustive, and you are certain to have many other and different adversities. What is important about this exercise is to identify what obstacles are impeding the realization of your dream. By creating a list, you will obtain an understanding of the number of adversities that need to be solved and overcome. Also, when you categorize the obstacles as internal or external, you will understand how many obstacles you truly have control over. Most of your internal adversities can be resolved with an internal choice and self-discipline. External adversities may require careful planning, persuasion, influence and precise execution to overcome.

As you set out to pursue your dream, create a list of all known internal and external adversities to overcome.

ADVERSITY MAGNITUDE CONTINUUM

MANAGEABLE   OVERWHELMING

ADVERSITY MAGNITUDE CONTINUUM

The meaning you attach to an adversity,
dictates the magnitude of adversity.

This is a part of the process where things become interesting and possibly abstruse. The adversity is not the real obstacle. The meaning you choose to attach to the adversity is the obstacle. This is an individual choice each and every one of us will make about whether we can or cannot manage an adversity. The Adversity Magnitude Continuum (AMC) ranges from *manageable* on one end to *overwhelming* on the other end.

In other words, the largeness, complexity or difficulty of any adversity is merely a mental construct. If you believe the adversity to be huge and crushing, it will be. If you believe the adversity to be manageable and navigable, it will be. You have a decision to make at this point – either the adversity will or will not be too much for you.

You must decide that adversity is manageable and you have the ability to overcome it. This is your choice, and it is a habit that successful people master and exercise often.

Let's dig deeper into this concept in the context of learning to ride a bicycle. Different people will have different adversities when trying to realize this dream. Listed below are some hypothetical adversities that may be encountered in this effort.

- I don't have a bicycle.
- I don't live near a safe place to learn to ride a bicycle.
- I live in a place that has snow & ice 9 months of the year.
- I have vertigo and trouble keeping my balance.
- I broke my back and have limited leg strength.
- I'm blind.

Let's look at each adverse circumstance in turn, to better understand how adversity is sized on the Adversity Magnitude Continuum.

<u>I don't have a bicycle.</u>
Perhaps this is not much of a problem if you're comfortably middle-class and can afford to spend $100 on a new bicycle. You choose to attach minimal meaning to the adversity, and it is manageable. You will overcome this adversity by going to the store and buying a bicycle. What if your finances were different, and you cannot afford to go out and buy a new bicycle? Perhaps, you will need to ask a neighbor to borrow a bicycle. What if you also suffered from socio-phobia, the fear of people and socializing, and don't talk to your neighbors; therefore, you cannot ask them to borrow a bicycle? In the second situation, it is easy to understand how you may choose to attach more meaning to the adversity, thereby making it overwhelming. Perceived personal circumstances are often a key component when choosing how much meaning to give any particular adversity.

<u>I don't live near a safe place to learn.</u>
Perhaps you live in Manhattan, New York where there are taxis and streets are filled with cars, sidewalks are filled with people and alleys have hazards that you may crash into. Or, you may live in an area in the mountains where there are no flat paved roads and the majority of terrain are uneven jeep roads. You may live on a boat with your family and are sailing from port to port. Each one of these scenarios presents a different perceived environmental component to the adversity. How do you size this adversity for the three different environmental scenarios? Based on background, the magnitude of the adversity will differ from person to person. The adversity is the same; however, to each individual person, the magnitude of the adversity can and does differ.

<u>I live in a place that has snow and ice nine-months of the year.</u>
Perhaps you were born and raised in Hawaii and just moved to the mountains in Ruka, Finland, where there is snow nine-months of the year, and the winter darkness suffocates the light of the sun. Or, you could be a native Finn who is accustomed to the winters and cleared snow and ice your entire lifetime. A Hawaiian and Finn are sure to attach different meanings to this same adversity.

<u>I have vertigo and trouble keeping my balance.</u>
Perhaps you had a car accident, and as a result have developed vertigo and experience a severe lack of balance. You are very cautious and only walk when you can balance yourself by holding onto someone or something. Alternatively, perhaps you are the only

professional tightrope walker who suffers from vertigo.

In the first car accident scenario, you may attach moderate to significant meaning to the adversity as you are in the process of rehabilitating from a car accident. You are trying to walk longer distances independently and want more of a challenge so you take on the additional dream of learning to ride a bicycle. In the second tightrope walker scenario, you may attach minimal meaning to your vertigo and balance issues in relation to learning to ride a bicycle. You are a professional tightrope walker and routinely confront and overcome this adversity as part of your livelihood. The more you confront and overcome the same adversity, the less meaning you will attach to it.

<u>I broke my back and have limited leg strength.</u>
Perhaps you became a Paralympian who won a gold medal in the marathon in the wheelchair division, and you continue to rehab your legs as you believe you will be able to walk again someday. I assume that a person who has broken their back, started wheelchair racing and achieved world champion level status would give less meaning to a broken back with limited leg strength than a couch potato who has the same injury (but maybe I'm wrong and it is the other way around). We individually choose how much meaning to attach to any particular adversity, and that decision can change from month to month, week to week, day to day, hour to hour or minute to minute. It is a personal decision to rate any adversity as *manageable* or *overwhelming*.

<u>I'm blind.</u>

Perhaps you were born without eyes, have a bicycle, live in a safe place that you can learn to ride a bicycle, the weather is good year-round, your balance is perfect, and your leg strength is sufficient – no problem, right?

The meaning you attach to an adversity
dictates the magnitude of adversity.

Your attitude about adversity is the difference between something that is manageable or overwhelming. It cannot be overstated that *attitude is everything*. The magnificent thing about attitude is that it is a decision we have full control over. Decisions can be made in an instant, and thus, our attitudes maintain the intrinsic characteristic to shift in an instant.

"How can I manage and change my attitude?" you may ask. The next section will explain how to do this.

MANAGING THOUGHTS

If you think your adversities are too hard and numerous, you will feel overwhelmed, and you may choose to stop pursuing your dream for this very reason. The flip side is that you may choose to think your adversities are manageable, in which case you will feel confident and choose to continue pursuing your dream. In order to achieve your dream, you need to take action (behave a certain way) to overcome adversity. So how do thoughts relate to and translate into behavior?

BEHAVIOR MODEL

+ ⟶ + ⟶ +

- ⟶ - ⟶ -

THOUGHTS   EMOTIONS   BEHAVIOR

There are numerous psychological theories for what influences behavior, and the purpose here is not to debate them. My purpose is to give you a tool to influence your own behavior in order to overcome your adversities. There is a basic psychological model for behavior that states thoughts drive emotions, which in turn drive behavior. A nuance of this is that positive thoughts drive positive emotions, which drive positive behavior (the "positive sequence"). The converse is true as well; negative thoughts drive negative emotions, which drive negative behavior (the "negative sequence").

In terms of sizing adversity, if you choose to think a specific adversity is manageable, you will have a feeling of confidence, and you are likely to behave such that you work to overcome the adversity. On the other hand, if you choose to think a specific adversity is overwhelming, you may feel inadequate and scared, and are likely to engage in behavior that does not overcome the adversity.

If you have negative thoughts and emotions, you are capable of re-engineering your thoughts and changing the resultant behavior. Once you realize you are thinking negatively and feeling negative, choose to stop the process. Have discipline and choose not to behave according to those negative thoughts and emotions. Instead, choose to re-engineer or restate your negative thought into positive thought patterns. This will then drive positive emotion and positive behavior.

RE-ENGINEER BEHAVIOR

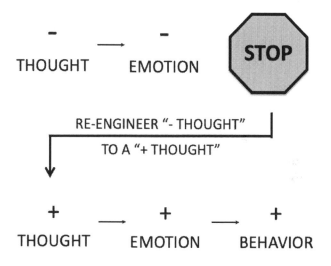

As you attempt to learn to ride a bicycle, you will use this process and size each obstacle on the Adversity Magnitude Continuum. If a specific adversity is sized as overwhelming, you should re-engineer the negative thought and resulting emotions. One of the internal adversities we presumed was that you had limited spare time to learn to ride a bicycle. If you believe your lack of time will prevent you from learning to ride, you may feel frustrated, disappointed or overwhelmed. The negative thoughts and emotions will likely result in the negative behavior of abandoning your dream to learn to ride a bicycle. If, however, you have negative thoughts and emotions and intervene before behavior takes place, you have a chance to re-engineer the negative sequence to become a positive sequence resulting in positive behavior.

Your task is to reframe how you choose to perceive the adversity of having limited spare time. If you only have 5 minutes of spare time a day, then re-think how you look at the situation. If you practice 5 minutes each day for a week, that is 35 minutes. If you practice 5 minutes every day for one month, that is 150 minutes or 2 and a half hours of practice. Two and a half hours of practice should be able to result in good experience and habits in the pursuit of learning to ride a bicycle. In thinking about the situation this way, you will view 5 minutes per day as a manageable amount of time to devote to the accomplishment of your dream, and you will feel confident, which in turn will drive a positive behavior of daily practice. In order for you to re-engineer a thought, you need to practice self-awareness in order to know when a negative thought is occurring.

RE-ENGINEER ADVERSITY

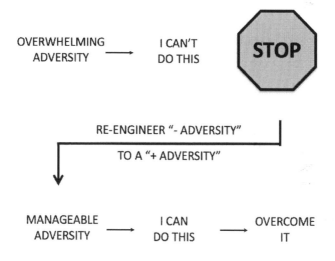

You can re-engineer the negative sequence at the thought stage, emotion stage or behavior stage. It is better to catch negativity earlier in the process and re-engineer it to a positive thought, as you will sacrifice time and energy as negativity transitions from thought to emotion then behavior.

By mastering this technique, you will possess the ability to transform adversity from being overwhelming into something manageable.

FACE YOUR FEAR EXCEPTION

Re-engineering thoughts may seem straightforward; but if you don't seem to have the ability to re-engineer a negative thought for some reason, then this exception is for you. Many people struggle with the ability to change thought patterns. Sometimes thoughts get stuck in our head, and anxiety arises when one attempts to change a thought. For these instances, you will use the *face your fear exception*. In this scenario, you have a negative thought AND negative emotion, but you choose to exhibit positive behavior. In psychological circles, this is commonly known as exposure therapy and part of dialectical behavior therapy. You think it's a bad idea, you're scared of it, but you do it anyway.

FACE YOUR FEAR EXCEPTION

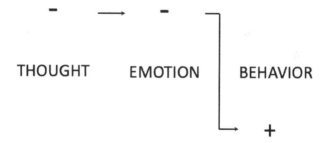

THOUGHT   EMOTION   BEHAVIOR

You only have 5 minutes to spare each day to learn to ride a bicycle. You feel overwhelmed by life and the thought of learning something new feels paralyzing. Despite this negative thought and emotion, you get on the bicycle 5 minutes each day and wobble around until you learn to ride. The face your fear exception takes immense self-discipline and courage; although it is short in duration. This exception is actually a decision, and decisions only take one second to make. Weighing perceived consequences in anticipation of making a decision is what takes time. In the face your fear exception, you do not bother with weighing consequences and you choose to behave in a manner that will overcome whatever adversity is in the way of your dream.

Face your fear to influence your future.

4

ADAPT

Adapt to change and change to adapt.

Congratulations! You made it through a very difficult phase of realizing a dream. You made a decision to believe in a thought and birth your dream. Then, you realized there are many obstacles standing in the way of your dream, and you chose to continue believing in your thought. You battled with your mind to re-engineer negative thoughts into positive thoughts. And you may have had to choose to just face your fear despite having negative thoughts. You are now at the second tripartite of The Success Cycle – the Adaptation Phase.

PLAN YOUR WORK & WORK YOUR PLAN

Benjamin Franklin - one of the founding fathers of the United States, writer, philosopher, scientist and inventor of the lightening rod and bifocals – is credited with saying:

Failing to plan is planning to fail.

ADAPT

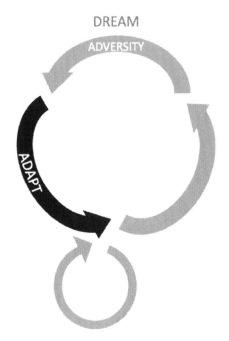

Dreams are not realized by just believing in a thought and randomly swashbuckling from one adversity to the next. It is necessary to create a plan to overcome each adversity; then, follow through and implement the plans with precision. This section will describe the two parts of the adaptation phase – plan & implement.

After you decided to believe you are going to learn to ride a bicycle, you need to create a plan for how you will learn this new skill. You will figure out a way to get access to a bicycle, and set aside time to practice. You may recruit a person who already knows how to ride a bicycle to help instruct you. Once you have created a plan for how to learn to ride a bicycle, you will follow through on it.

IMAGINE, INNOVATE, IMPROVISE

This is the part of The Success Cycle where your creativity gets to reign free. You can generate and brainstorm a plethora of ideas to overcome adversities by yourself or enlist the help of others. In order to develop a solid strategy, you should use the "3 I's" of planning – *imagine, innovate* & *improvise.*

Imagine. Use your imagination to *think of brand-new ways of doing something.* This is true "out of the box thinking." There are no constraints on your ideas, and they may never have been tested or used by you or others. They are novel strategies to overcome what is inhibiting your dream. Nothing can limit your thoughts and ideas.

Innovate. Take existing ideas, tools or systems and modify them to suit your purposes. There are plenty of things already in existence, which can be extremely useful if you just tweak them a little. Innovation is a great approach to conserve time, energy and resources. Your task is to customize the idea, tool or system to help you overcome your adversities.

Improvise. To improvise is to *use what is readily available in different ways* on an ad hoc basis. Improvisation assumes a more extemporaneous and on the fly approach to planning. As you create a plan, you may find that there is a "gap" or a missing piece of your plan. With all your best efforts, you are just unable to determine how to get from point A to B. In this instance, you will rely on your abilities to improvise and come up with a solution in the moment.

Draft a plan on paper or computer with two columns. In one column, list out each adversity that is inhibiting your dream. In the other column, use the 3 I's to create strategies to overcome the adversity. You may use one or all of the 3 I's to create your plan to overcome each adversity, see the following table as an example.

It is mission critical to create and document the plan. The bigger your dream, the more adversities you will have, and the larger and robust your plan must be. The more difficult or novel an adversity is, the more "I's" you must use to overcome it. In other words, if it is a simple adversity, perhaps you can innovate and overcome it. If the adversity is extremely difficult and novel, you may need to use imagination, several types of

USE 3 I'S TO ADAPT

Adversity	3 I's
1.	Imagine: Innovate: Improvise
2.	Imagine: Innovate: Improvise:
3.	Imagine: Innovate: Improvise:

innovation and improvise many times. Your decision about what strategies to implement will be driven by your own perceptions of Cost-Benefit Planning. Cost-Benefit Planning for purposes of The Success Cycle describes the situation where you weigh the perceived effort involved to implement strategies against the perceived consequence of failing to overcome the adversity on this attempt.

The perceived effort to implement strategies can include physical labor, consumption of resources including time and money, the strain the strategy may cause to relationships, and a whole host of other factors. It is important to understand you are estimating or forecasting the "effort" you think will be involved in implementing a strategy. Once you actually implement a strategy, the effort involved could be more, less or the same as you estimated. Also, if your dream consumes joint resources of a partner, you should anticipate the possibility of a disconnect. Make sure partners are bought into your dream as much as you are, if you are using their resources to fund your dream. An alternative is to discuss the potential for disconnect in advance so the relationship and/or dream is not derailed.

The perceived consequence of failure is what you believe will happen if your dream is not achieved, and the value you place on that circumstance. Remember this is only a prediction of what you think will occur, which may or may not come to fruition. Integral to this analysis is the subjective value that you place on the emotional impact of failure. Stated another way, "How bad do you want to avoid failure?"

COST–BENEFIT PLANNING

PERCEIVED
EFFORT TO
IMPLEMENT
STRATEGIES

PERCEIVED
CONSEQUENCE
OF FAILURE

Each of us go through a Cost-Benefit Planning process consciously or sub-consciously as we develop and decide which strategies to use to overcome adversity. Invest your time wisely and spend adequate time creating a solid plan. You will thank yourself later.

There are no short cuts for success.

As you create a plan to learn to ride a bicycle, you will create strategies to overcome adversities. In Chapter 3 of this book (Adversity), hypothetical internal and external adversities were identified. They have been listed on the next page, and plans created for how to overcome each adversity using imagination, innovation and/or improvisation.

The plans are not exhaustive and intended to demonstrate that for any adversity, you can use imagination, innovation and/or improvisation to develop strategies. Also, there are countless possible ideas for how to overcome each of the listed adversities, and that is the beauty of this exercise.

We get an opportunity to look at each adversity individually and create a unique and specific plan for how to overcome it. The more people with whom you have brainstormed, the more ideas and strategies will be generated. After you have brainstormed ideas, you will engage in Cost-Benefit Planning with all of the ideas that were generated and assess the effort to implement strategies against the perceived consequence of failure.

Adversity	3 I's
Lack of time to practice	Imagine: Dedicate 5 minutes per day to practice riding a bike. 5 minutes over 30 days is 2.5 hours of practice time. Innovate: Re-purpose half of your daily exercise time to learning to ride a bike. Improvise: When you wake up early or have unexpected time free up in your schedule, use it to learn to ride a bike.
Poor balance	Imagine: Ask somebody to help balance the bike while you practice. Innovate: Use training wheels when practicing. Improvise: Use an indoor exercise bike trainer to keep your balance while your muscles get accustomed to peddling and having your body in a biking position.
Scared to crash and be hurt	Innovate: Use a helmet, handguards, leg guards or any other protective gear you have around your home. Wear jeans and a long sleeved shirt to help prevent skinning your body in the event of a crash. Improvise: Choose a softer surface than concrete or asphalt, such as a rubberized running track at a nearby school.
No safe place to learn	Imagine: Think about places where there are no cars, with low traffic and no obstacles to crash into – a parking lot or park with a protected area for bicycles. Also, consider the time of day when there is low traffic in this area. Innovate: Perhaps you'll block off a section of an alley way, or paved area, to ensure you can peddle safely with no through traffic.
It is winter and cold outside	Imagine: Brainstorm and find an indoor area to learn. Postpone your learning until the weather warms. Innovate: Dress warm. Improvise: Be spontaneous and when the weather is at it's warmest during the day, change your schedule and dedicate time to learn to ride a bicycle.
Flat tire	Imagine: Learn how to fix the tire by reading an article or watching a YouTube tutorial. Ask a neighbor to teach you how to fix it. Take the bicycle to a bike shop to fix the flat tire. Improvise: Borrow a working bicycle from a neighbor.

To illustrate this point, let's look at the first adversity listed above – lack of spare time to learn to ride a bicycle. There were several strategies that could be used to overcome this adversity using imagination, innovation and improvisation.

> Imagine: Dedicate 5 minutes per day to practice riding. Five minutes over thirty days is 2.5 hours of practice time.

> Innovate: Re-purpose half of your daily exercise time to learning to ride.

> Improvise: When you wake up early or have unexpected time free up in your schedule, use it to learn to ride.

It is a personal decision whether to use one or a combination of strategies. You will use Cost-Benefit Planning to make this decision. For each strategy or combination of strategies, you should assess the effort involved to implement the strategy and compare it against the perceived consequence of failure. Your imagination strategy of setting aside 5 minutes every day to practice could be perceived as a high level of effort, as you may feel overwhelmed and like you don't have a minute to spare. The competing considerations are whether you feel this is a valuable use of 5 minutes per day, and what you determine are the consequences of not learning to ride a bike on this attempt. This is a very personal decision that boils down to – *how badly do you want your dream to be realized at this point?* If your very existence hinges on the fulfillment of this dream, then you will implement every strategy that you have brainstormed, as the perceived consequence of failure is unacceptable. There is no universal right or wrong in Cost-Benefit Planning. Your decision will be right for you under the circumstances. This exercise is intended to give you a framework for how to decide which strategies to use in order to overcome any given adversity.

It is also critical to accept that these are postulated theories you are testing. And, inherent in testing theories is the fact that theories can be effective, or not. At this point, you're halfway through the Adaptation Phase.

IMPLEMENT

A superb plan is insignificant until it is implemented.

The second half of the Adaptation Phase is all about implementing the plan you developed in the first half of the phase. You will take the plan you created and methodically implement it with discipline and precision. This is called operational excellence in many industries. Your commitment to your dream and mettle are going to be tested at this stage. Up to this point, you have done a lot of mental and emotional work. This is the part of The Success Cycle where your dream is working and trying to enter the material world.

Your job is to take your plan and implement each strategy exactly as you planned it. This sounds easy, but it takes a lot of discipline to do each step of a plan exactly how it is planned. You're sure to run into temptations and alluring situations where you think you can take a shortcut.

There are no shortcuts for success.

Do the work exactly as you planned it, even if it is hard, time consuming, uncomfortable or hurts. It has been postulated that humans are innately "lazy" and prone to conserving energy, so when they need to go on a hunt, they will have adequate energy stores. Whether this theory is accurate or not, the truth is that it is easier *not* to do work than it is to do work. And so, the temptation of taking a shortcut in your plan, or taking a day off, or not following through on every step of your plan become real barriers to precise implementation, and the realization of your dream.

You must choose to relentlessly implement and execute your plan as it was developed. You must choose to have the discipline and drive to follow through on all of your strategies. Operational excellence is about having the mindset to leave no stone unturned, to ensure every detail and step is followed, and to know that you have done absolutely everything in your power to follow through with your strategy as planned.

When plans are implemented with operational excellence, you will know for certain whether the plan was effective in overcoming the specific adversity. When a strategy is not executed with precision and shortcuts are taken, one of two things happens – either the plan overcomes the adversity or it does not. If the latter occurs, there is uncertainty about whether the plan was effective or deficient. The plan may very well have been an effective strategy to overcome adversity, but you will not know for certain because it was not implemented with exactitude. It is worth repeating a pragmatic aphorism again.

There are no shortcuts for success.

In your effort to learn to ride a bicycle, you developed several strategies to overcome adversities. This is the point where you must follow through on the strategies and do exactly what was planned. In the prior example, three possible strategies were brainstormed to overcome a lack of time to practice riding a bicycle. Let's assume you planned to overcome this adversity by choosing to implement all three strategies based upon Cost-Benefit Planning.

Adversity	3 I's
Lack of time to practice	*Imagine*: Dedicate 5 minutes per day to practice riding. Five minutes over thirty days is 2.5 hours of practice time. *Innovate*: Re-purpose half of your daily exercise time to learning to ride. *Improvise*: When you wake up early or have unexpected time free up in your schedule, use it to learn to ride.

In order to achieve operational excellence, it is necessary to enlist work ethic and discipline to follow through with each strategy until the plan is implemented as envisioned. You will schedule a daily 5-minute block into your calendar to practice and you must respect it.

Second, you will repurpose half of your 1 hour of daily exercise (or 30 minutes) to your dream, learning to ride a bicycle. Set an alarm, so you know when half of your exercise time is complete and it is time to transition to pursuing your dream. Finally, whenever you have a cancellation or free-time in your schedule, dedicate this time to learning to ride a bicycle. On a daily basis, you are certain to practice riding a bicycle for 35 minutes; and periodically, you may get more time if you wake up early or appointments cancel. As you can imagine, you will need to be extremely disciplined and vigilant to follow-through on these strategies for a long period of time.

Diligent follow through will set you apart from the crowd and communicate excellence.
- John Maxwell

And this is where "talkers" and "doers" are separated. Many times in life, you will encounter people who talk a good game, but when the time comes to roll up the sleeves and do what was talked about, they mysteriously disappear or stop contributing. If you are a doer, you're naturally wired to follow-through with your plans. If you're a talker, you may notice you talked a lot about your dream, created grandiose strategies and you have difficulty hunkering down to implement the plan you made for yourself. When it comes to pursuing your dream, a delegation of tasks usually is not an option. If you are a talker the good news is, you can literally change and become a doer in one second. Make the decision to be a doer, and start doing. It will feel unnatural at first, but you are capable of following through on your strategies.

The adaptation phase is all about creating and implementing a plan.

5

"THE CRUX"

crux / noun/ - An essential point requiring resolution.

The Success Cycle and the pursuit of your dream inevitably arrive at a point I call *The Crux*. This part of the process occurs immediately after the adaptation phase. Your plans and their implementation will either overcome the adversities associated with your dream, or they will not. If your dream is large, complex, novel and difficult, it is not uncommon to initially fail to overcome all of the adversities. The result is failure and you will not achieve your dream on your first attempt. When you fail, you enter the Resilience Loop. If your adaptations overcome all the adversities, you will achieve your dream (*discussed in Part 7: ACHIEVE*).

After you created and implemented your plan to learn to ride a bicycle, either you will have learned to ride or not. If you learned to ride, you will have achieved your dream and completed a cycle through The Success Cycle. For purposes of discussion, let's assume you implemented your plan with precision and did not learn to ride.

"THE CRUX"

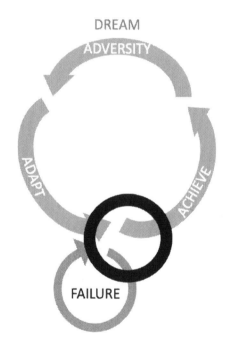

FAILURE So you failed in your attempt to achieve your dream. No biggie. If you think about success in a linear fashion, you may think your journey is over, which may become a crisis situation. However, if you choose to shift your paradigm and think of success as cyclical, you will understand that failure is only a part of the process. For epic dreams, you should expect to fail many times. Some really gifted and extraordinary people understand that the only path to real success is through failure.

Failure is success in progress.
- Albert Einstein

Successful people don't fear failure,
but understand that it's necessary
to learn and grow from.
- Robert Kiyosaki

Failure is the opportunity
to begin again.
- Henry Ford

Success consists of going from failure to failure
without loss of enthusiasm.
- Winston Churchill

I've failed over and over again in life, and that is why I succeed.
- Michael Jordan

In great attempts, it is glorious even to fail.
- Bruce Lee

Every time you fail,
you are one step closer to succeeding.
- Jason Romero

Failure and success are not mutually exclusive concepts. Rather, *failure is an implicit part of the cycle of success.* You are not a failure because you fail. After you pick yourself back up from a failure, you can be certain that you are on the right path to succeeding. Struggle builds character.

Extraordinary people
are borne from
extraordinary struggle.

6

RESILIENCE LOOP

Failure is just the beginning.

It is a common misconception that an effort or attempt is over after a failure. We may wish it to be the case because of high emotions or exhaustion; however, this is far from the truth. I often say *failure is just the beginning*. There is much to be gained from failure, as long as you understand it is just a part of the cycle of success.

Failure ignites resilience, and resilience is the stuff that forges champions, pioneers and heroes. I define resilience as *the ability to recover from hardship and difficulty*. It is a trait that is highly revered and sought after in the workplace, and it is rare to encounter in a culture where being comfortable is prized. The good news is, resilience is a process that can be taught and learned. In terms of The Success Cycle, resilience is a sub-process.

The Resilience Loop has three (3) notable components – the Stop Sign, Growth and Re-adaptation.

RESILIENCE LOOP

THE STOP SIGN - PAIN & FEAR

After a failure, you are likely to experience two strong emotions that can feel paralyzing - pain and fear. Pain is a feeling that happens in the *present* moment. Fear is a feeling about something that could happen in the *future*. Pain and Fear can paralyze the pursuit of your dream. How can you overcome the paralyzing forces of pain and fear? This section will teach you a simple process you can use to overcome each emotion.

Pain may manifest itself in many forms, including physical, financial or emotional pain. The important thing to remember about pain is that it is felt in the present moment. It has nothing to do with the past or the future. It is all about the present moment, and that can make it a very overwhelming feeling. When your pain is great, it seems like it could go on forever and you may worry that its intensity will increase indefinitely. You will wonder how you can continue on in this amount of pain.

There are some basic truths about pain that we need to understand. Truth #1 - Pain is temporary. Although it may seem like our pain will continue indefinitely, it will not. Eventually, we will get relief from pain. Truth #2 - If we fight pain, we lose. When we focus on pain and fight with it, we give it energy, strength and prolong its existence. Truth #3 - You can overcome pain. The way to overcome pain is simple. You acknowledge the pain, and you accept it. In other words, you admit that you have pain and that's just the way it is. Once you acknowledge and accept pain, you transcend it and can again begin making forward progress to accomplish your dream.

Fear is an emotional reaction about the future, something that has yet to occur. This can be a very strong emotion that can be paralyzing after a failure. As with pain, this emotion can be overcome with a simple technique. When an emotion sabotages and entices you to drift into the future, you can overcome it by distracting your mind and returning to the present. In relation to fear, the easiest way to derail it is to practice gratitude. Gratitude is all about being present with positive thoughts. On the contrary, fear is all about the future and negative thoughts. When you practice gratitude in the face of fear, you distract your mind and reclaim your power to persevere. Think about what you are fearing, then think about something you are grateful for despite having fear. For example, I have a degenerative eye disease and am fearful about losing the light perception I still have. In the face of that fear, I am grateful for having the opportunity to see colors, appreciate beautiful sunrises and sunsets, and marvel at the faces of my children. My fear of total darkness vanquishes when I am grateful for what I currently have.

It takes time to learn to acknowledge and accept pain, and practice gratitude in the face of fear. These skills are learned through repetition. Don't expect to be perfect on the first try; and, you may need to acknowledge and accept the same pain and express gratitude day after day until it sticks. This is not something you can rush, but if you are consistent and intentional in practicing acknowledgment and acceptance, and gratitude daily, you will achieve mastery of these skills. This mastery will permit you to overcome the Stop Sign that exists within failure, now and in the future.

<u>PAIN</u> Let's return to the dream of learning to ride a bicycle. Assume you tried to ride in a parking lot, lost balance and crashed on asphalt. Your left knee and elbow were bruised, scraped and bled. You were unsuccessful at The Crux and are now at the Stop Sign of pain and fear.

Your knee and elbow exude excruciating pain, and gravel is lodged in those areas. You also see dripping blood from your knee and elbow, which is alarming. As you scoot yourself out from under the fallen bicycle to stand up, you realized that your hand also feels bruised. You are experiencing significant physical pain. The feelings you experience are in the present moment. As you stand up and focus on the pain in your knee, elbow and hand, the pain seems to grow in intensity and transforms from a throbbing to shooting pain. The more focus that is given to the injuries, the more opportunity pain has to grow. Pain has overwhelmed you at this moment and paralyzed you in your attempt to learn to ride. The way to reclaim your power is to acknowledge and accept pain. You simply stop and acknowledge that you have become injured, and you accept the fact that your hand, elbow and knee hurt and are bleeding. You stop fighting pain and you acknowledge and accept your situation. When you do this, you will overcome the paralyzing characteristic of pain. REMEMBER: This is a skill that needs to be practiced over and over to gain mastery. You may need to do this every few minutes if you feel the pain is severe.

FEAR After your epic crash, it would be common for you to also experience fear. As you lay on the ground bleeding with your bicycle on top of you, you will contemplate whether you should get up and try again. Fear will try to stop you and paralyze the pursuit of your dream. Fear will sabotage your mind, and you may start daydreaming about future crashes that might happen if you try again. Your next crash may result in the other side of your body being scraped up. Then you would have twice the amount of excruciating pain. Or, maybe your next crash would result in a broken bone, and maybe that bone could penetrate the skin. Or worse yet, maybe the next crash would result in a brain injury that would leave you in a coma for months. You can see how fear tries to sabotage your mind. Your thoughts are about something in the future that has yet to occur. As you lay on the ground with a skinned hand, elbow and knee, your fear is attempting to paralyze the pursuit of your dream. The paralyzing force works because you have let your mind travel into the future of possible negative outcomes. Fear stops the pursuit of our dreams because it feeds our mind's negative thoughts about things that could happen in the future.

The simple way to overcome fear is to come back to the present with positive thoughts and practice gratitude. Expressing gratitude is the act of being thankful. An example of expressing gratitude after your crash would be to feel thankful for having a bicycle, for having two arms and legs that work and permit you to learn this

UNPARALYZE

EMOTION	ERA	STRATEGY TO OVERCOME
PAIN	PRESENT	ACKNOWLEDGE & ACCEPT
FEAR	FUTURE	GRATITUDE

skill without additional hardship, for having sustained minor injuries that don't require hospitalization, for living in a country where you have freedom and the spare time to learn to ride a bicycle, and so on. When you fill your mind and heart with gratitude, there is no room for fear. *Fear cannot paralyze if you are grateful.* In psychological terms, you have distracted your mind from having negative thoughts about the future to having positive thoughts about the present. REMEMBER: practicing gratitude is a skill. The more we do it, the more proficient we become at it. The more grateful you are, the more positive and present you will become. Grateful people are good to be around, and they are people who accomplish incredible things.

In summary, after a failure, you will experience pain and fear. These emotions will attempt to paralyze and force you to give up on your dream. Overcoming pain and fear is part of resilience and integral to the process of success. The way to overcome pain is to acknowledge and accept it. You must practice this skill time and again in order to gain proficiency. The skill does not miraculously vanquish the feeling of pain, but it sterilizes the paralyzing nature of pain. Fear will attempt to sabotage your mind with negative thoughts and take you into the future of possibilities. The way to overcome fear is through gratitude - having positive thoughts and returning to the present. Practicing gratitude is a proven method to overcome fear. Again, practicing gratitude is a skill and will take time to become proficient. As you gain mastery in the art of acknowledging and accepting pain and practicing gratitude in the face of fear, the Stop Sign will become a Yield Sign where you will merely slow down; and eventually, the sign may totally disappear.

GROWTH – STRENGTH AND WISDOM

We grow more from summits never achieved.

After you fail and decide to continue on, you will grow in two significant ways. You will grow *stronger* and *wiser.* Strength and wisdom are two mandatory components of resilience. Strength is the capacity to withstand and ability to exert force or pressure. Strength is built by doing the same motion over and over with increased force or pressure. Think of failure as being a metaphor for falling down. Every time you get back up, you use muscles in your arms and legs. After doing this one-thousand times, those muscles will necessarily become stronger as you have used them over and over. The same process occurs with your emotions every time you choose to try again after a failure. The emotions you need to continue on become stronger every time you choose to try again.

Wisdom is a body of knowledge that is accumulated through experience and study. Every time you fail, you must analyze your failure and understand why it occurred. First, you should analyze the plan you developed to see if there was a flaw or opportunity for improvement. Then, you should analyze the implementation of your plan and determine whether it was implemented with 100% precision. Perhaps there was an unexpected circumstance that you were unable to plan for with the experience you had at the time. Only after attempting to implement your plan was the circumstance revealed. In other words, you had to fail in order to have a chance at succeeding. As long as you analyze each failure and determine why the failure occurred, you will be growing wiser. Your body of knowledge, experience and study of your situation will increase. Hence, failure is an incredible opportunity to grow wiser.

Resilience Quotient: The great phenomenon about resilience is that it is cumulative and can be generalized. The experience of failing and trying again makes you more apt to try again in future failures. This can be mathematically calculated for data-driven people. For each time in life that you failed and tried again, your strength and wisdom quotient will increase by 1. Combined, I call this the Resilience Quotient. Mathematically, you could see that you will be stronger and wiser after four (4) failures, as compared to your first failure. After your first failure, your Resilience Quotient is only 2 – strength rating of 1 plus a wisdom rating of 1. After your fourth failure, your Resilience Quotient is 8 – strength rating of 4 plus wisdom rating of 4. You can see that your cumulative Resilience Quotient grows by a factor of 2 for each failure.

FAILURE	STRENGTH RATING	WISDOM RATING	RESILIENCE QUOTIENT
1	1	1	2
2	2	2	4
3	3	3	6
4	4	4	8

For all the times you have failed in life and chosen to continue on, your Resilience Quotient has increased by a factor of 2. This is cumulative for all failures in all streams of life, including personal and professional pursuits. Resilience is also grown from enduring difficult circumstances in life and choosing to go on despite the circumstance.

Resilience is what makes ordinary people extraordinary.

For example, if you have experienced struggle and failure in your personal life and chosen to try again and again, you will have a high Resilience Quotient. When you step into a professional setting, you may realize that you are very different from your peers, who may not have experienced the amount of failure and struggle. The difference is your Resilience Quotient is extremely high relative to your cohort. You have grown your resilience through the experience of rebounding from personal failure and struggle. You will apply this in a professional setting, and your approach and ability to rebound from failure will be significantly different and superior to peers without as many failures and struggles.

Take for example, the true story of Chris Gardner, a single-father. He was homeless with his toddler child, accepted an unpaid internship with a stock brokerage firm in San Francisco where only one intern would be offered a paid job at the end of the 6-month internship. Gardner experienced eviction, was jailed for unpaid parking tickets, had his bank account garnished by the

RESILIENCE QUOTIENT EXAMPLE

	Chris Gardner			Other 19 Interns		
Failure / Struggle	Strength	Wisdom	Resilience Quotient	Strength	Wisdom	Resilience Quotient
No College	1	1	2	0	0	0
Single Parent	2	2	4	0	0	0
Eviction	3	3	6	0	0	0
No Income	4	4	8	0	0	0
Homeless	5	5	10	0	0	0
Arrested for unpaid parking tickets	6	6	12	0	0	0
IRS garnishes bank account	7	7	14	0	0	0
Work Failure 1	8	8	16	1	1	2
Work Failure 2	9	9	18	2	2	4
Work Failure 3	10	10	20	3	3	6
Work Failure 4	11	11	22	4	4	8

IRS for unpaid taxes, showed up for meetings and work without showering and in worn clothing, and more. It could be said that each hardship, or failure, made Gardner grow stronger and wiser, increasing his Resilience Quotient. When he applied himself in a professional setting, it was apparent that he was stronger and wiser than the other 19 interns, many of whom had Ivy League educations and privileged backgrounds. Gardner's Resilience Quotient was the difference. He experienced much struggle and failure in his life, and he chose to keep trying – which meant he was growing his Resilience Quotient. The preceding chart is an exemplar of how Gardner's Resilience Quotient compared against the 19 other interns at the brokerage firm who did not have Gardner's amount of hardship and failure. We do not know the exact story of the other 19 interns, and I'm sure each of them had hardship and failure as well. The chart is meant to illustrate the concept that rebounding from successive struggles and failures throughout one's life creates a much higher Resilience Quotient.

What is important to note is that one's Resilience Quotient can only be grown through experience with failure and struggle; it cannot be grown by reading a book, attending a seminar, graduating from a specific university or paying a certain amount of money. Resilience is the true "x-factor" of The Success Cycle.

The more you fail, the more likely
you are to succeed.

If you continue to fail, that necessarily means you are continuing to try, which is a very good thing. If you continue to try and fail over and over again, you are growing your Resilience Quotient. And people with a high Resilience Quotient are able to accomplish incredible feats. This is because they do not quit when they fail. They learned that failure is an opportunity to better themselves. They have learned that failure is just part of the process of succeeding.

Let's return to the dream of learning to ride a bicycle. You just crashed due to a loss of balance and lay on the ground with a hurt hand, and bloodied elbow and knee. You think about what caused the crash, decide to stand up, pick up the bicycle, mount it and prepare to make another attempt. What happened?

While you were on the ground, you thought about what caused you to crash – a loss of balance. You wobbled so much that you fell over. You believed you were going so slow that this increased your wobbliness. You choose to try a second time and crash. You think you need to peddle faster to gain even more speed. You try a third time and crash, because you couldn't put both feet on the peddles before wobbling to a crash. The fourth time you try, you are able to peddle and gain enough speed to eliminate wobbliness and stay upright. However, this time you crash because you don't know how to stop. In these four failed attempts, you have grown your Resilience Quotient significantly.

	STRENGTH RATING	WISDOM RATING	RESILIENCE QUOTIENT
1	1	1	2
2	2	2	4
3	3	3	6
4	4	4	8

After you have crashed four times, your Resilience Quotient is 8. That is 75% higher than your Resilience Quotient after your first crash (which was 2). You have grown stronger physically and mentally every time you stood up after an unsuccessful attempt. Biologically, you exercised the muscles necessary to stand and mentally, you exercised the neuropathways necessary to try again after a failure. As discussed previously, after every failed attempt, you dissected the failure and learned what caused the failure to occur. You learned from the failure, and added that experience to grow your knowledge base and wisdom.

Because resilience is cumulative, you will be able to benefit in your professional life from your Resilience Quotient gained from attempting to learn to ride a bicycle. In other words, after a weekend of failed attempts to learn to ride a bicycle, you will enter the office with a higher Resilience Quotient than if you did not fail and try again. You increased your overall resilience in a different setting by failing and trying again.

RE-ADAPTATION

After a failure, you will find yourself returning to the

adaptation phase of The Success Cycle. You will analyze why the failure happened and determine whether it was caused by a faulty plan or imperfect implementation of the plan, or both. If the original plan was flawed, you will re-adapt and refine the plan based on your new wisdom gained in the Resilience Loop. If the implementation of your plan was imperfect, you will determine how to ensure your plan can and will be implemented with precision next time. If the plan and implementation were flawed, you will re-adapt and refine the plan and determine how to ensure your plan can and will be implemented with precision.

Let's return to your dream of learning to ride a bicycle. You made a plan, implemented it, crashed your bike, got back up and are ready to try again. Why did you crash, and how do you need to change your plan or the implementation of your plan so you successfully learn to ride? In the example we have been using, you fell because of being too wobbly. Let's assume that after you analyzed your plan, you believe you could benefit from the coaching of an experienced person who knows how to ride a bicycle. Also, you missed quite a few planned practice sessions. Go back to your original plan, and refine it. When you practice, you want to have an experienced bicyclist with you to observe your technique and give advice. Re-adapt your plan, and add that refinement. You also noted that the implementation of your plan was imperfect, i.e., you missed planned practice sessions. Find ways to hold yourself accountable to make 100% of your practice sessions – set an alarm, ask a friend to hold you accountable, or improve your self-discipline with a strategy that works for you.

With your new and improved plan, you will execute the plan and again head into The Crux. It is possible that you may fail again and repeat the Resilience Loop. You may need to do this several times. Don't be afraid or discouraged to fail and build resilience. Remember, every time you fail and continue trying, you are increasing your Resilience Quotient. And, the resilience you gain in learning to ride a bicycle can be generalized and applied at work, in relationships or a future dream. Eventually, your plan and its implementation will meet the mark, you will pass through The Crux and you will succeed in manifesting your dream. In this, you must choose to believe and have faith.

7

ACHIEVE

Achieve what you believe.

Achievement of the dream is the final tripartite of The Success Cycle. Your dream may have been to learn to ride a bicycle, get a promotion, feel healthy or run across the United States. Whatever your dream was, you have finally manifested it into reality. Three important things happen when you arrive at the Achieve phase - manifestation, confidence and analysis.

Manifestation You need to stop and appreciate what you have accomplished. You transformed an intangible thought into a tangible reality. Some movies and books portray this as magic, supernatural or highly improbable. The fact is, you are capable of everything and anything. The Success Cycle is the process by which dreams, intangible thoughts, are transformed into reality, the tangible realm. Knowing that there is a process for success, understanding it and painstakingly working through the process is tantamount to achieving dreams.

ACHIEVE

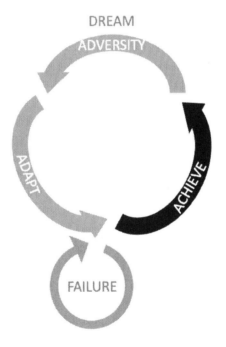

You are not a wizard, but many people may think you are magical. You are not a hero, but many people may think you have slayed dragons. You are not different than anybody else, but many may believe you are. You have completed The Success Cycle. And, we all successfully complete this process at different points in our lives. People tend to take notice when a dream is really hard, big or has never been accomplished before. I used this same process for learning to ride a bicycle, becoming a Paralympian and CEO, establishing and breaking world records, and running across a continent.

It is important for you to understand that you are capable of manifesting your dream into reality. That being said, it is more important for you to understand that you do not do this on your own – there is a process, you have helpers and something larger conspires to help you make your dreams come true.

Confidence As you achieve your dream, your confidence will grow. You will have the knowledge and belief that you can achieve incredible things. You will learn and believe that a process exists which can be followed to accomplish your wildest dreams. Confidence grows through time and experience with the process and amplifying one's Resilience Quotient. Your confidence will enable you to believe in epic thoughts and achieve the seemingly impossible.

Analysis A necessary part of achieving a dream is analyzing how you were able to navigate The Success Cycle. I encourage everybody to dissect the fulfillment of each dream into the different phases of The Success

Cycle. When did you have the initial thought? When did you choose to believe in your thought and make it a dream? How did you develop a plan with imagination, innovation and improvisation? What was your implementation plan? How did you do with the implementation of your plan? Did you drop into the Resilience Loop? Why? How did you overcome Pain and Fear? How did you become stronger and wiser? How did you refine and re-adapt your plan? How much time did you spend in the Resilience Loop? When did you achieve your dream? What did you learn from manifesting your dream? How has your confidence been affected?

We should learn as much or more from our accomplishments as our failures. The fact is, many times, we forget to analyze how we achieve goals. We look at achievement of a dream as the finish line, but it is not. Remember, success is cyclical and not linear.

Success is not final...
- Winston Churchill

As soon as you achieve your goal, you will begin dreaming again and preparing to enter The Success Cycle again, and again, and again.

8

PILLARS OF MENTAL STRENGTH

Within the mind are the seeds of success.

You may be asking yourself whether this process truly encapsulates how to succeed and if it can be learned and mastered. If this is true, won't everybody succeed in their dreams? This is my hope. However, it is not that simple. The same process is used by everybody, but not everybody continues to move through the process. Sometimes people choose to quit. People have many reasons for quitting – changing priorities, perceived difficulty, frustration and so on. Whatever the reason, they have permitted their dream to be hijacked. And, at some point in The Success Cycle we are all going to want to quit. It will be easier to stop than to continue trying. This is the point where champions and pioneers separate themselves from the masses.

The fuel that will keep you engaged in the pursuit of your dream throughout The Success Cycle are the 4 Pillars of Mental Strength. I experienced these pillars throughout my life, although they were revealed to me as

4 PILLARS OF MENTAL STRENGTH

PILLAR	ERA
HOPE	FUTURE
PATIENCE	PRESENT
CONSISTENCY	PRESENT
FORGIVENESS	PAST

I ran across America with limited eyesight, in a severe depression, separated from my children, destitute and on the verge of being hit by cars and semi-trucks. The pillars are: Hope, Patience, Consistency and Forgiveness. Each pillar is a choice, and so they become mental challenges. Mental strength is what fuels your progress from one part of the process to the next. It is developed over time and through practice. In order to make a muscle stronger, you exercise it. In order to make your mind stronger, you must also exercise it.

The Pillars operate most effectively in different eras of time. In other words, when you feel like quitting, ask yourself whether a thought about the past, present or future is trying to make you quit. If your thought is about the future, use Hope. If your thought is about the present, use Patience and Consistency. If your thought is about the past, use Forgiveness.

HOPE is about believing in something for which there is no evidence. It is about choosing to believe when you and others are doubtful, critical and unbelieving. Your experience and intellect may tell you something is impossible, but you choose to have Hope despite all the evidence and noise to the contrary. There will be times when you will lose Hope. In these times, you must make a conscious choice to have Hope. The easy path is to give up hope, quit and go home. Remember that success is just a process, and as long as you keep going through the process, you will eventually achieve your dream. Refuse to give up or give in.

As I ran across America, there were days when the only

thing I could do was cry. I couldn't hold my kids. I couldn't sleep in my bed. I didn't know whether I would live. All I could do was have Hope that I would be able to cross America on foot, and I would live to complete the journey. I had to choose to have Hope. I had many sabotaging throughs of doubt, and I had people telling me I was foolish and would fail.

The best time to use Hope is when the future looks dark and bleak. When your mind wanders into future negative possibilities, enlist the pillar of Hope. Make a choice to have Hope, and carry on toward the realization of your dream.

I choose to have Hope.

PATIENCE In the pursuit of dreams, as in my run across America, there will be storms. Sometimes those storms may last an hour or 3 hours, a day or 3 days. But, the truth about storms is that eventually, they will pass you by. When a storm is upon you during The Success Cycle, exercise patience. One day when I was running across America, I woke to a horrible rain and wind storm in Oklahoma. If I ran into the wind, I was barely moving faster than an easy walk; so, I decided to walk. I walked for 7 hours into a headwind that seemed like it would never cease. My goal was to travel 50 miles or more on foot within 12 hours. After 7 hours, I had only walked 20 miles. I was exercising patience and conserving energy as the storm was upon me. I was waiting for my opening, for the storm to break. The storm finally passed after 7 hours. I only had 5 hours to cover 30 miles. That meant I would have to average 10-

minute miles for 5 hours straight. I felt well-rested as I'd been walking for 7 hours. I started running. After 12 hours, I looked at my watch and I had achieved 50 miles for the day. Choose patience when the storm is upon you.

As you progress through The Success Cycle, you are certain to find yourself in a storm. Perhaps, you have been cycling through the Resilience Loop time after time. Conserve energy, choose to be patient and carry on. Eventually, the storm will pass you by. When we are in the midst of a tempest, they can seem indefinite; but they are not. Storms are finite, and they all have a beginning and an ending.

The best time to use Patience is when there is a challenge you are experiencing in the present moment.

Patience is power.

CONSISTENCY: If you make consistent effort toward your dreams daily, you will experience consistent results. The inverse is true as well; inconsistent effort equals inconsistent results. Consistent effort is possible despite external and internal environments. When I ran across America, I had a goal to run 50 miles or more every day. Every day, except for 2 days, I achieved 50 miles or more. On the first day I failed to achieve 50 miles, the support van drove on a flat tire in the desert and the tire was cut. We had to drive 50 miles to the nearest town and replace the tire, accumulating only 16 miles of running for the day. On the second day I failed to achieve 50 miles, I simply ran out of daylight.

CONSISTENCY

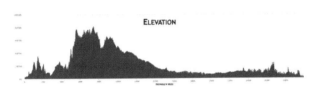

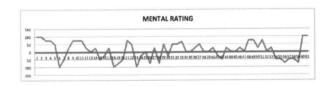

Because of my degenerative eye condition and severe night blindness, I committed to not run past sunset due to the danger of being hit by a vehicle. At sunset, I had achieved 48 miles after a day of torrential downpours and a couple of unexpected delays. Other than those two days, I achieved 50 miles per day or more. On the last two days, I ran 60 miles and 70 miles, respectively, and I did not take any days off.

The elevation profile in the graphic is intended to represent external factors that affect us, including other people, priorities and commitments. The mental rating is intended to represent internal states that we experience, including emotions like sadness, grief, elation, frustration and joy. The daily mileage bar chart is intended to demonstrate that a person is fully capable of exerting consistent effort and achieving consistent results despite fluctuating external factors and internal emotions.

Choose to be consistent in your effort. Consistency is best used when you are experiencing a challenge in the present moment.

Consistent effort is paramount.

FOREGIVENESS: This is the most powerful pillar of mental strength. It is often said that we are a product of our past. *Choosing forgiveness, is choosing to be free.*

As I spent 12+ hours running 50+ miles every day across America, I had a lot of time to think. For the first few days, I replayed my life several times, and I was fairly grateful for the life I had lived. It didn't take long, however, for the negative thoughts to creep into my head. I found myself reliving events that had hurt me. Why did I lose that job? Why did certain relationships have to fail? Why did that person hurt me? Why did I have to go blind? My mental mindset was deteriorating, and I was becoming a victim. It took 1,500 miles of running to get to a point where I could find nobody else to blame for all my hurt, despair and problems.

And then, it became very serious. I had to look at myself for what I am and am not. I had to see myself with all my frailties and faults. I had to accept and acknowledge that I had hurt people and done things of which I was ashamed. When I finally arrived at this point, I realized I needed to forgive myself for what I had done and what I had failed to do. Once I took that step, I was finally able to begin working on forgiving other people.

Forgiveness of others happens after forgiveness of self.

When we forgive ourselves and others, we shed a tremendous burden of emotional baggage. I ran stronger and faster after my experience with forgiveness (and 1,500 miles of running). The mental and emotional baggage had weighed me down significantly. It slowed and distracted me from the pursuit of my dreams. Once I jettisoned the emotional baggage with forgiveness, I was laser-focused on my dreams and progressing through The Success Cycle.

Forgiveness is best used to neutralize negativity that is associated with the past.

In summary, when you feel like quitting at any stage in The Success Cycle, use the Pillars of Mental Strength to stay in the game. If you become a master at choosing to practice hope, patience, consistency and forgiveness, you will find that you quit less, achieve more, and feel empowered.

9

BIOLOGICAL IMPERATIVES

Care for your body to care for your dream.

There are four biological imperatives that humans must respect in order to accomplish great things. They are simple yet significant. The first imperative is *sleep*. Seven to eight hours of sleep per night is critical for peak physical and mental health. Insufficient sleep can negatively impact mood, appetite, health and in rare cases, can cause death. The second imperative is *hydration*. Sixty-percent of the human body is water and more than 70% of the brain, heart and lungs are water. It is estimated that in the United States, 75% of people are chronically dehydrated. Lack of hydration can lead to high blood pressure, kidney stones, fatigue, memory issues, anxiety bouts and more. Simply stated - drink water. The third imperative is to *eat well*. Your body needs calories to function, repair and grow strong. Consume an appropriate amount of good food to help your body perform. Moderate the amount and type of food you consume. The fourth imperative is *exercise*.

BIOLOGICAL IMPERATIVES

S.H.E.E.

SLEEP

HYDRATE

EAT WELL

EXERCISE

Exercise your body for an hour each day. This can take the form of a brisk walk, calisthenics, bike riding, weight training, yoga, dance or any other form of movement that requires muscle and cardiovascular exertion. These biological imperatives are foundational for people who want to consistently succeed in transforming their dreams into manifested realities. An entire book could be written on these biological imperatives.

CONCLUSION

It is my dream that by sharing The Success Cycle, you will understand the awesomeness of the power you possess. You will begin to know that absolutely everything and anything is possible. At your core, you will begin to truly believe that you are capable of all things. And now your charge is to use this process, and teach and encourage others to accomplish their dreams. The gift of this book is intended to be shared with all, not to be hidden or used selfishly. I humbly ask you to be a steward of this process. Implement it again and again in your own life. Teach your children, co-workers, and anybody who is at a loss of understanding why their life did not turn out as they wanted it to.

You can have the life you desire. The choice is yours, and the power to transform your dream into reality is within you, waiting to be harnessed and unleashed into this world.

Let there be peace in all that you pursue.

The Beginning

AFTERWARD

Success to Significance

Once you have become a master of The Success Cycle, you will find that your dreams evolve and become more externally focused. Instead of having dreams for personal pursuits, you will dream about goals that impact others, the community and the world at large. When your dreams are "we focused" instead of "me focused," you will be taking part in a different process, The Significance Cycle. The only difference between The Success Cycle and The Significance Cycle is the focus of your dream.

I sincerely hope that we are all able to move from the pursuit of success to significance.

Dream EPIC!

The Success Cycle

ABOUT THE AUTHOR

Jason is an expert on success and resilience, a coach and an international keynote speaker. He is the only blind person to run across America (a top-10 fastest foot-crossing at 51.5 miles/day), holds more than 10 World Records in extreme endurance athletics, has competed internationally for Team USA at the Paralympic World Marathon Championships, is the subject of a full-length documentary, *Running Vision*, is an author and a pioneer for ultra-running for the blind and visually impaired. In addition to being an ultra-endurance athlete, he has been a CEO, attorney and led and founded non-profit organizations that serve youth. He is on a mission to encourage, inspire and teach people how to realize their dreams.

To inquire about booking Jason for speaking engagements, coaching services and media inquiries, please visit www.jasonromero.net.

BOOKS BY JASON ROMERO

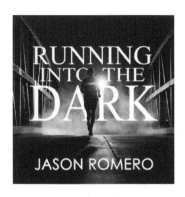

The memoir of a 3,063-mile sprint across America.

"I learned that my blindness did not make me disabled. I am not broken. I have been forced to develop a limitless amount of adaptability, resilience from failure, grit and perseverance as a result of my challenge.

I learned that pursuing a passion relentlessly will bring out the best in a person. I learned that there is more good than bad, more help than hurt, and more light than dark.

I learned that love never fails, and because of that, absolutely everything and anything is possible."

- Jason Romero (Running into the Dark)

THE SUCCESS CYCLE

---

workbook

notes:

BIOLOGICAL IMPERATIVES

Step 1: Make the decision today to: i) sleep 7-8 hours per night, ii) hydrate with water (1 gallon per day), iii) eat well in moderation, and iv) exercise 1 hour per day.

Step 2: Follow through.

BIOLOGICAL IMPERATIVES

S.H.E.E.

SLEEP

HYDRATE

EAT WELL

EXERCISE

notes:

PILLARS OF MENTAL STRENGTH

Step 1: Commit not to quit on your dream.

Step 2: Re-read the section on the Pillars of Mental Strength.

Step 3: When you get the urge to quit, use one or all of the 4 Pillars of Mental Strength to continue moving through The Success Cycle.

4 PILLARS OF MENTAL STRENGTH

PILLAR	ERA
HOPE	FUTURE
PATIENCE	PRESENT
CONSISTENCY	PRESENT
FORGIVENESS	PAST

notes:

DREAM

Step 1: Write down a *thought* (goal) you have for your life?

_____

_____

_____

Step 2: Do you *believe* your *thought* will be a reality for you?

_____ Yes (the only real answer)

_____ No

CONGRATULATIONS! You have a dream to chase.

Your dream is your perfection

THOUGHT

+

BELIEF

=

DREAM

notes:

ADVERSITY

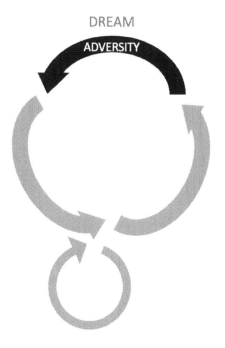

notes:

ADVERSITY MAGNITUDE CONTINUUM

MANAGEABLE   OVERWHELMING

notes:

ADVERSITY

Step 1: Identify and list all adversities to your dream. Categorize them as Internal/External to you or your organization.

Step 2: For each adversity, classify it as Manageable (M) or Overwhelming (O)

Internal Adversities	M/O
_____	____
_____	____
_____	____
_____	____
_____	____
_____	____
_____	____

External Adversities	M/O
_____	____
_____	____
_____	____
_____	____
_____	____
_____	____
_____	____

notes:

BEHAVIOR
MODEL

+   ⟶   +   ⟶   +

-     ⟶   -   ⟶   -

THOUGHTS   EMOTIONS   BEHAVIOR

notes:

RE-ENGINEER BEHAVIOR

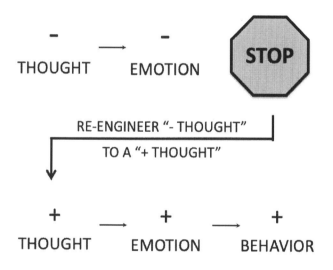

notes:

RE-ENGINEER
ADVERSITY

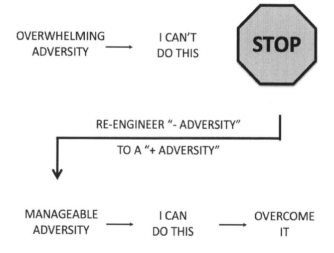

notes:

FACE YOUR FEAR EXCEPTION

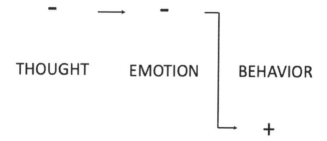

notes:

OVERWHELMING ADVERSITY

Step 1: For all adversities that are Overwhelming and have a negative sequence Behavior Model, re-frame the adversity to a positive sequence.

Step 2: For any adversity which you are unable to re-frame into a positive sequence, choose to implement a Face Your Fear Exception (FYFE).

Step 3: List all adversities you will need to implement a FYFE.

FYFE Adversities

_____
_____
_____
_____
_____
_____
_____
_____
_____
_____
_____
_____

notes:

ADAPT

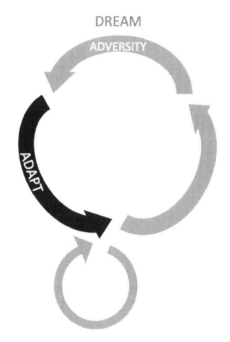

notes:

ADAPT (part 1) – create a plan

Step 1: For each adversity, imagine, innovate and improvise theoretical ways to overcome the adversity. Use a spreadsheet or piece of paper to create your plan.

Step 2: Perform a Cost-Benefit Analysis for each adversity and assess the perceived effort to implement the strategies against the perceived consequence of failure on this attempt.

Step 3: Determine which strategies you will implement for each adversity.

USE 3 I'S TO ADAPT

Adversity	3 I's
1.	Imagine: Innovate: Improvise
2.	Imagine: Innovate: Improvise:
3.	Imagine: Innovate: Improvise:

notes:

COST–BENEFIT PLANNING

PERCEIVED EFFORT TO IMPLEMENT STRATEGIES

PERCEIVED CONSEQUENCE OF FAILURE

notes:

ADAPT (part 2) – implement a plan

Step 1: Implement your plan with methodical precision. Do not take any shortcuts.

notes:

"THE CRUX"

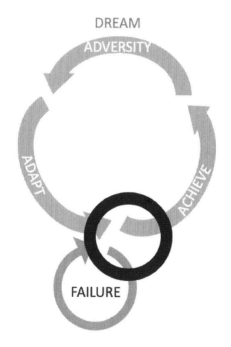

notes:

"THE CRUX"

Step 1: Did you achieve your dream? If yes, skip this section and the Resilience Loop section.

Step 2: If you failed to achieve your dream, move to the next section on the Resilience Loop

Step 3: Read and repeat the following,

Failure is success in progress
- Albert Einstein

notes:

RESILIENCE LOOP

PAIN
FEAR

FAILURE

STRENGTH & KNOWLEDGE

notes:

RESILIENCE LOOP

Step 1: Identify whether you are feeling Pain and/or Fear after your failure. Pain is a feeling about something that is present and it can take the form of financial, emotional, physical and mental pain. Fear is a feeling about something in the future that has yet to occur.

Step 2: For any pain you are feeling, *acknowledge & accept* it and carry on.

Step 3: For any fear you are feeling, reframe the situation and express gratitude for an aspect of your failure. This mental distraction will bring your mind back to the present and enable you to neutralize fear and carry on.

Step 4: Assess whether you implemented your plan with perfect precision. If not, implement the plan again, this time precisely as planned.

Step 5: If the plan was implemented with precision and a failure occurred, that means the plan was deficient in some way. Dissect and analyze why the plan failed to meet its intended purpose.

Step 6: Use the 3 I's to brainstorm more strategies to overcome the adversities. Revise your plan with these new strategies, and implement the new plan.

notes:

UNPARALYZE

EMOTION	ERA	STRATEGY TO OVERCOME
PAIN	PRESENT	ACKNOWLEDGE & ACCEPT
FEAR	FUTURE	GRATITUDE

notes:

RESILIENCE QUOTIENT (RQ)

Step 1: Assess your resilience quotient. Count the number of failures, major setbacks and traumatic events you have overcome in your life. Multiply this number by 2. *Worksheet provided on next page.*

Resilience Quotient	Level
0-6	Fair
6-10	Good
10-20	High
20-30	Exceptional
30+	Super Star

Step 2: Choose to try again

notes:

RESILIENCE QUOTIENT WORKSHEET

Failure, Trauma, Struggle	Strength	Wisdom	Resilience Quotient
	1	1	2
	2	2	4
	3	3	6
	4	4	8
	5	5	10
	6	6	12
	7	7	14
	8	8	16
	9	9	18
	10	10	20
	11	11	22
	12	12	24
	13	13	26
	14	14	28
	15	15	30
	16	16	32
	17	17	34
	18	18	36
	19	19	38
	20	20	40
	21	21	42
	22	22	44
	23	23	46
	24	24	48
	25	25	50

notes:

ACHIEVE

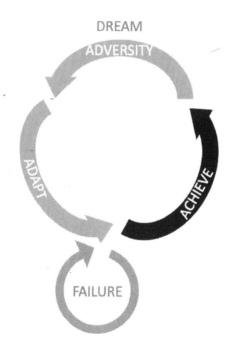

notes:

ACHIEVE

Step 1: Relish in what you have accomplished, and let it feed your self-confidence. You have transformed an intangible thought into a manifested reality.

Step 2: Analyze how you succeeded. What parts of The Success Cycle process felt natural and unnatural to you? Have you mastered sizing adversity, managing thoughts, developing and implementing plans, overcoming pain & fear? Have you mastered the biological imperatives and the pillars of mental strength?

Step 3: Repeat & *DREAM EPIC!*

notes:

THE SUCCESS CYCLE

transform dreams into reality

BIOLOGICAL IMPERATIVES
SLEEP
HYDRATE
EAT WELL
EXERCISE

PILLARES OF
MENTAL STRENGTH
HOPE
PATIENCE
CONSISTENCY
FORGIVENESS

DREAMS

ADVERSITY

MANIFESTATION
IMAGINE   CONFIDENCE
INNOVATE   ANALYSIS
IMPROVISE
IMPLEMENT

ADAPT

ACHIEVE

PAIN
FEAR

"THE CRUX"

RESILIENCE
LOOP

FAILURE

STRENGTH & KNOWLEDGE

ACKNOWLEDGEMENTS

Alone we can do so little,
together we can do so much
- Helen Keller

Writing a book is a very difficult endeavor; and this work was created in a particularly challenging time in my life. It is with great gratitude and humility that I thank a small village starting with God, *thank you for everything*!

Family & Friends:
To Sofia, your kind heart, words and actions have inspired me time and again to not give up or give in on this book, my dreams and life.
To Sage, every day you demonstrate and model true resilience and kindness.
To Sierra, for challenging me to grow, evolve, dream and think deeply in the face of injustice and rectification of the same.
To Mom, who has supported and modeled The Success Cycle for me for as long as I can remember.
To Fred, you supported and gave me a chance to become all that I could be, I love you and our time

together was cut far too short.

To Dad, I have become the man I am partly because of you, and for that I am grateful.

To Troy, you are my one and only blood brother, and we will always have each other.

To David Pierce, you showed up and loved me when it mattered most....thank you!

To East Phillips, for decades of friendship through many seasons of life, I always know you're in my corner and that means everything.

To Schaef, who never gave up on, challenged and prayed for me, and taught me that God is good all the time.

To Gregg Carson, the way you live life has taught me that resilience is limitless and available to us all.

To Todd Schiff & Bryan Lawrence, for more than four decades of growing, doing life together and caring for one another, you taught me that not all brothers are related by blood.

To Jay Flynn, for the countless miles we have traversed together on foot, by car and emotionally, you are very important to me.

Business:

To Team Puerto Rico at GE – Carmen, Debbie, Desiree, Dottie, Eric, Jorge, Jose, Ketty, Lidia, Lourdes, Mayiya, Otto, Rosy, Yvonne and all our employees, we lived The Success Cycle over and over, and demonstrated time and again that small teams can deliver big results with consistency. Puerto Rico lo hace mejor!

To Dennis Markusson, who mentored and taught me well when I was a young attorney.

To Frances Draper, who took a chance on and gave me

the opportunity to embark on a business career. I never imagined where it would lead, the experiences I would have or the challenges I would be forced to grow from. Thank you for believing in me.

To Professor Giles Bateman, thank you for sharing your expertise and passion for business pursuits to inspire myself and many other students at the University of San Diego.

To Margaret Keane, a leader who truly cares about people and driving results with integrity. Thanks for giving me a chance and sending me to Puerto Rico – they were formidable and great years of learning, leading and living.

To Jeff Sommer, for all the talks we had about leadership, business, life, problems and solutions; and your sage piece of advice, "always take the high road, it's the right place to be in running, business and life."

Athletics:

To Scott Gordon, my running sensei whose humility, support and zest for getting *out there* has inspired me to run headfirst without fear to *the edge*.

To Mark Lucas, for believing in my dream and standing behind me when nobody else would.

To Luigi Dessy, a person who helped me learn that the real adventure in running is not finishing a race, it is journeying together.

To Camilo Martinez, for your inspiring spirit of knowingly running into total devistation, then digging deep, exercising resilience and finding a way to stay in the race and finish.

To Valmir Nunes, for demonstrating and teaching me the heart of a true champion.

To Marshall Ulrich, for your friendship, support, encouragement and AMAZING accomplishments that have inspired me to dream EPIC.

To Ted Epstein, you are simply *the man* to me. I know you're enjoying a well-deserved rest now.

To Ken Clouber & Merilee Maupin, for letting me cut my teeth in Leadville and your supportive and encouraging mission to teach us all that "we are better than we think we are, and we can do more than we think we can."

To the International Spartathlon Association, that taught me sometimes failure is the best and purest path to success; and, that life doesn't owe us a thing.

Blindness:

To Richard Hunter, who helped restore my vision when eyesight failed me.

To Luanne Burke, who has guided me into a life of blindness, and taught me how it is done with courage, grace and authentic emotion.

To Adrian Broca, who has been a hero of mine because of his heart, integrity and athleticism.

To Aaron Scheidies, who revealed and demonstrated over and over that crushing athletic performances can be realized by blind people.

Inspiration:

To Sir Ernest Shackleton, a kindred spirit who never quit on his team, was the human embodiment of *never losing Hope* and risked everything for the greater good.

To Dr. Wayne Dyer, whose soothing words, thoughts and perspectives have course-corrected my heart time and again.

To the 14th Dalai Lama, thank you for your wisdom and peaceful thought.

To Mother Theresa, whose life, light and spirit inspires me daily to serve.

To Ghandi, who challenged me to be the change I want to see in the world.

To Sir Ken Robinson, author of *The Element*, whose work and life has posited unconventional decisions as the opportunity for aptitude and passion to collide.

To M. Scott Peck, author of *The Road Less Travelled*, which has been a literary work that has taught, challenged and guided me throughout life to be brave and journey in a way I believe has great meaning.

Be kind

www.jasonromero.net